Francis Frith's
South East London

Photographic Memories

Francis Frith's
South East London

Leigh Hatts

FRITH
BOOK Co

First published in the United Kingdom in 2002 by
Frith Book Company Ltd

Hardback Edition 2002
ISBN 1-85937-494-8

Paperback Edition 2002
ISBN 1-85937-263-5

British Library Cataloguing in Publication Data

Francis Frith's South East London
Leigh Hatts

Frith Book Company Ltd
Frith's Barn, Teffont,
Salisbury, Wiltshire SP3 5QP
Tel: +44 (0) 1722 716 376
Email: info@francisfrith.co.uk
www.francisfrith.co.uk

Printed and bound in Great Britain

AS WITH ANY HISTORICAL DATABASE THE FRITH ARCHIVE IS CONSTANTLY BEING CORRECTED AND IMPROVED
AND THE PUBLISHERS WOULD WELCOME INFORMATION ON OMISSIONS OR INACCURACIES

Contents

Francis Frith: *Victorian Pioneer*

FRANCIS FRITH, Victorian founder of the world-famous photographic archive, was a complex and multi-talented man. A devout Quaker and a highly successful Victorian businessman, he was both philosophic by nature and pioneering in outlook.

By 1855 Francis Frith had already established a wholesale grocery business in Liverpool, and sold it for the astonishing sum of £200,000, which is the equivalent today of over £15,000,000. Now a multi-millionaire, he was able to indulge his passion for travel. As a child he had pored over travel books written by early explorers, and his fancy and imagination had been stirred by family holidays to the sublime mountain regions of Wales and Scotland. 'What a land of spirit-stirring and enriching scenes and places!' he had written. He was to return to these scenes of grandeur in later years to 'recapture the thousands of vivid and tender memories', but with a different purpose. Now in his thirties, and captivated by the new science of photography, Frith set out on a series of pioneering journeys to the Nile regions that occupied him from 1856 until 1860.

Intrigue and Adventure

He took with him on his travels a specially-designed wicker carriage that acted as both dark-room and sleeping chamber. These far-flung journeys were packed with intrigue and adventure. In his life story, written when he was sixty-three, Frith tells of being held captive by bandits, and of fighting 'an awful midnight battle to the very point of surrender with a deadly pack of hungry, wild dogs'. Sporting flowing Arab costume, Frith arrived at Akaba by camel seventy years before Lawrence, where he encountered 'desert princes and rival sheikhs, blazing with jewel-hilted swords'.

During these extraordinary adventures he was assiduously exploring the desert regions bordering the Nile and patiently recording the antiquities and peoples with his camera. He was the first photographer to venture beyond the sixth cataract. Africa was still the mysterious 'Dark Continent', and Stanley and Livingstone's historic meeting was a decade into the future. The conditions for picture taking confound belief. He laboured for hours in his wicker dark-room in the sweltering heat of the desert, while the volatile chemicals fizzed dangerously in their trays. Often he was forced to work in remote tombs and caves where conditions were cooler. Back in London he exhibited his photographs and was 'rapturously cheered' by members of the Royal Society. His reputation as a photographer was made overnight. An eminent modern historian has likened their impact on the population of the time to that on our own generation of the first photographs taken on the surface of the moon.

Venture of a Life-Time

Characteristically, Frith quickly spotted the opportunity to create a new business as a specialist publisher of photographs. He lived in an era of immense and sometimes violent change. For the poor in the early part of Victoria's reign work was a drudge and the hours long, and people had precious little free time to enjoy themselves. Most had no transport other than a cart or gig at their disposal, and had not travelled far beyond the boundaries of their own town or village. However,

by the 1870s, the railways had threaded their way across the country, and Bank Holidays and half-day Saturdays had been made obligatory by Act of Parliament. All of a sudden the ordinary working man and his family were able to enjoy days out and see a little more of the world.

With characteristic business acumen, Francis Frith foresaw that these new tourists would enjoy having souvenirs to commemorate their days out. In 1860 he married Mary Ann Rosling and set out with the intention of photographing every city, town and village in Britain. For the next thirty years he travelled the country by train and by pony and trap, producing fine photographs of seaside resorts and beauty spots that were keenly bought by millions of Victorians. These prints were painstakingly pasted into family albums and pored over during the dark nights of winter, rekindling precious memories of summer excursions.

The Rise of Frith & Co

Frith's studio was soon supplying retail shops all over the country. To meet the demand he gathered about him a small team of photographers, and published the work of independent artist-photographers of the calibre of Roger Fenton and Francis Bedford. In order to gain some understanding of the scale of Frith's business one only has to look at the catalogue issued by Frith & Co in 1886: it runs to some 670 pages, listing not only many thousands of views of the British Isles but also many photographs of most European countries, and China, Japan, the USA and Canada – note the sample page shown above from the hand-written *Frith & Co* ledgers detailing pictures taken. By 1890 Frith had created the greatest specialist photographic publishing company in the world,

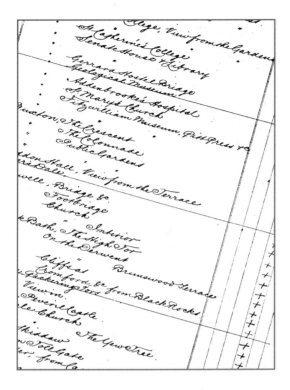

with over 2,000 outlets – more than the combined number that Boots and WH Smith have today! The picture on the right shows the *Frith & Co* display board at Ingleton in the Yorkshire Dales. Beautifully constructed with mahogany frame and gilt inserts, it could display up to a dozen local scenes.

Postcard Bonanza

The ever-popular holiday postcard we know today took many years to develop. In 1870 the Post Office issued the first plain cards, with a pre-printed stamp on one face. In 1894 they allowed other publishers' cards to be sent through the mail with an attached adhesive halfpenny stamp. Demand grew rapidly, and in 1895 a new size of postcard was permitted called the court card, but there was little room for illustration. In 1899, a year after

Frith's death, a new card measuring 5.5 x 3.5 inches became the standard format, but it was not until 1902 that the divided back came into being, with address and message on one face and a full-size illustration on the other. *Frith & Co* were in the vanguard of postcard development, and Frith's sons Eustace and Cyril continued their father's monumental task, expanding the number of views offered to the public and recording more and more places in Britain, as the coasts and countryside were opened up to mass travel.

Francis Frith died in 1898 at his villa in Cannes, his great project still growing. The archive he created continued in business for another seventy years. By 1970 it contained over a third of a million pictures of 7,000 cities, towns and villages. The massive photographic record Frith has left to us stands as a living monument to a special and very remarkable man.

Frith's Archive: *A Unique Legacy*

FRANCIS FRITH'S legacy to us today is of immense significance and value, for the magnificent archive of evocative photographs he created provides a unique record of change in 7,000 cities, towns and villages throughout Britain over a century and more. Frith and his fellow studio photographers revisited locations many times down the years to update their views, compiling for us an enthralling and colourful pageant of British life and character.

We tend to think of Frith's sepia views of Britain as nostalgic, for most of us use them to conjure up memories of places in our own lives with which we have family associations. It often makes us forget that to Francis Frith they were records of daily life as it was actually being lived in the cities, towns and villages of his day. The Victorian age was one of great and often bewildering change for ordinary people, and though the pictures evoke an impression of slower times, life was as busy and hectic as it is today.

We are fortunate that Frith was a photographer of the people, dedicated to recording the minutiae of everyday life. For it is this sheer wealth of visual data, the painstaking chronicle of changes in dress, transport, street layouts, buildings, housing, engineering and landscape that captivates us so much today. His remarkable images offer us a powerful link with the past and with the lives of our ancestors.

Today's Technology

Computers have now made it possible for Frith's many thousands of images to be accessed almost instantly. In the Frith archive today, each photograph is carefully 'digitised' then stored on a CD Rom. Frith archivists can locate a single photograph amongst thousands within seconds. Views can be catalogued and sorted under a variety of categories of place and content to the immediate benefit of researchers.

Inexpensive reference prints can be created for them at the touch of a mouse button, and a wide range of books and other printed materials assembled and published for a wider, more general readership - in the next twelve months over a hundred Frith local history titles will be published! The day-to-day workings of the archive are very different from how they were in Francis Frith's time: imagine the herculean task of sorting through eleven tons of glass negatives as Frith had to do to locate a particular sequence of pictures! Yet

THE FRANCIS FRITH COLLECTION

Photographic publishers since 1860

HOME | PHOTO SEARCH | BOOKS | PORTFOLIO | GALLERY   MY CART
Products | History | Other Collections | Contact us | Help?

your town, your village

365,000 photographs of 7,000 towns and villages, taken between 1860 & 1970.

The Frith Archive
The Frith Archive is the remarkable legacy of its energetic and visionary founder. Today, the Frith archive is the only nationally important archive of its kind still in private ownership.

The Collection is world-renowned for the extraordinary quality of its images.

The Gallery
This month The Frith Gallery features images from "Frith's Egypt".

the FRITHgallery

News...
Image update complete. An additional 5,000 images have been added and the quality of all images has now been improved.

Sample Chapters avaliable. The first selection of sample chapters from the Frith Book Co.'s extensive range is now available. All are offered in Pdf format for easy downloading and viewing.

explore FRITH
Search thousands of photographs from one of the worlds' great archives.

Town search
GO

County search
Select a county
GO

See Frith at www.francisfrith.co.uk

the archive still prides itself on maintaining the same high standards of excellence laid down by Francis Frith, including the painstaking cataloguing and indexing of every view.

It is curious to reflect on how the internet now allows researchers in America and elsewhere greater instant access to the archive than Frith himself ever enjoyed. Many thousands of individual views can be called up on screen within seconds on one of the Frith internet sites, enabling people living continents away to revisit the streets of their ancestral home town, or view places in Britain where they have enjoyed holidays. Many overseas researchers welcome the chance to view special theme selections, such as transport, sports, costume and ancient monuments.

We are certain that Francis Frith would have heartily approved of these modern developments in imaging techniques, for he himself was always working at the very limits of Victorian photographic technology.

The Value of the Archive Today

Because of the benefits brought by the computer, Frith's images are increasingly studied by social historians, by researchers into genealogy and ancestory, by architects, town planners, and by teachers and schoolchildren involved in local history projects.

In addition, the archive offers every one of us an opportunity to examine the places where we and our families have lived and worked down the years. Highly successful in Frith's own era, the archive is now, a century and more on, entering a new phase of popularity.

The Past in Tune with the Future

Historians consider the Francis Frith Collection to be of prime national importance. It is the only archive of its kind remaining in private ownership and has been valued at a million pounds. However, this figure is now rapidly increasing as digital technology enables more and more people around the world to enjoy its benefits.

Francis Frith's archive is now housed in an historic timber barn in the beautiful village of Teffont in Wiltshire. Its founder would not recognize the archive office as it is today. In place of the many thousands of dusty boxes containing glass plate negatives and an all-pervading odour of photographic chemicals, there are now ranks of computer screens. He would be amazed to watch his images travelling round the world at unimaginable speeds through network and internet lines.

The archive's future is both bright and exciting. Francis Frith, with his unshakeable belief in making photographs available to the greatest number of people, would undoubtedly approve of what is being done today with his lifetime's work. His photographs, depicting our shared past, are now bringing pleasure and enlightenment to millions around the world a century and more after his death.

South East London - *An Introduction*

SOUTH EAST LONDON begins deep in central London. Many buildings in SE1 on the south bank of the River Thames are further north than Buckingham Palace and the Houses of Parliament in so-called 'central London' on the north bank. Indeed, Southwark Cathedral is further north than Westminster Abbey.

This division of London into north and south of the River Thames derives from early times when the capital was only on the north bank. The City of London, later joined by the City of Westminster, looked across the water at a string of riverside country estates which were deemed to be not in

London, but in Surrey. These estates were the Bishop of Winchester's residence in his Diocese of Winchester, which then embraced the land along the River Thames; a detached part of the Duchy of Cornwall; and Lambeth Palace, where the Archbishop of Canterbury lived to be handy for the Royal Palace of Westminster and Parliament opposite. Southwark Cathedral is the successor to the priory built alongside the Bishop of Winchester's house; this stood near St Mary Overie Dock, which is featured in this book. These great south bank estates and hamlets all looked to Kent and the south-east. Indeed, Lambeth Palace is built

on land swopped with an estate in Kent's Darenth Valley.

St Thomas Becket visited Southwark Priory on his last trip to London from Canterbury just weeks before his murder in 1170. In the years that followed, pilgrims would set out to Becket's shrine at Canterbury from the many pubs nearby in Borough High Street. This is because London Bridge was the only river crossing, and so Kent-bound travellers tended to converge on Southwark and make sure that they were over the bridge from London before the gates closed at night. Inns offering accommodation here did well. Later, the Kentish hops were brought to Southwark, where the Hop Exchange in Southwark Street and Borough Market still exists.

Today, London Bridge Station is the gateway to Kent and Canterbury for pilgrims, tourists and commuters. But London's boundary now embraces so much of old Kent that many commuters, and even tourists, alight within south-east London - even if the ambience is rural Kent, as it is at Old Bexley or Bromley.

But before arriving at the new outer London boroughs, there are the old suburbs of Camberwell and Peckham. These were reached by way of the Elephant & Castle; we see it in this book in the 1890s, when both the road junction and the pub looked very different. Today, the Elephant & Castle is being treated to a multi-million-pound regeneration scheme. It is interesting that the modern Elephant

& Castle public house is following the example of the original by offering accommodation. The pub was once a farrier's, and coaches leaving from here could reach Mickleham below Box Hill in an hour.

The Elephant may be unrecognisable today, but just down Walworth Road it is exciting to find that Camberwell has not changed so much; it still has many buildings around the green which can be found in the historic photographs. It also has a surprise, for the landmark bank building survives. Many people still pass through its doors - but above the doorway the word 'bank' has become 'surgery'. The nearby Old Kent Road had a pub which has also turned into a surgery.

There are big changes along Camberwell Road at Peckham, where a shopping centre has claimed half the now pedestrianised street. Just south of here, but still in the London Borough of Southwark, is Dulwich village; here, very little has changed. However, even here it is the new shop fronts which have succumbed to modernisation. Dulwich Park may seem unchanged too, but a close look at the rowing boats today will reveal more modernisation and a lighter structure.

The neighbouring community of Herne Hill still has many of its old shops - the butcher, the pie shop, the greengrocer's and even the laundrette are in the same place as in the fifties. However, Dulwich's other neighbour, Forest Hill, has suffered the loss of two very prominent churches. It is therefore surprising that the cinema has just been

saved to be a pub: the bar replaces the stage, and the old low lighting has been retained. Best of all, in the circumstances, is the retention of the cinema's name as recognition that the building is a local landmark.

The London Borough of Lewisham touches the Thames at Deptford. To the south of Lewisham, where the church dates from Tudor times, is the hamlet of Southend, where a remaining pond recalls the days when the water powered a mill. Indeed, today's main road has grown from a narrow lane flanked by ditches. This reminds us that south-east London is a collection of joined-up villages on the road to London, or nearby old centres of government such as Greenwich or even Eltham.

Greenwich owes its present world-famous look to Charles II, who gave up the old palace there for the beautiful buildings of the Royal Navy and the Royal Astronomer. Earlier, it had been a favourite palace of the Tudors, but Henry VIII would often retreat to nearby Eltham Palace for Christmas. There St Thomas More was made Lord Chancellor. Behind Eltham today is Mottingham village, which maintains in a rural atmosphere the fine Porcupine pub, a shopping street, and a popular working stables.

Not far south is Chislehurst. Its parish church was built on the profits of 'Hymns Ancient & Modern' by the vicar Canon Francis Murray, who helped to influence both the revival of music and liturgy in the Church of England. Nearby is a

woodland, and here soon afterwards another man had influence far beyond both Chislehurst and south-east London. Early in the 20th century, William Willett was riding in Petts Wood when he had the idea of Summer Time - moving the clocks forward one hour in the summer. Petts Wood is rare in being a London woodland protected by the National Trust.

Much of the employment until the early 1960s was in such places as Erith to the east of the reclaimed land which is now Thamesmead. At Erith the change in streetscape is most remarkable. The High Street has almost disappeared, along with the crowds which seem to inhabit the old photographs. Today the new concrete shopping centre often appears empty, bereft of big shops or even once-familiar names such as Boots, which used to have a presence here. Morrisons supermarket on the quay is now the only building which attracts any substantial traffic. Here is an example of how valuable the Frith archive is in reminding us of change and recording lost buildings.

In nearby Old Bexley, a Frith photograph confirms that after a disastrous fire the local mill has been restored to at least look like the old building, even if it is now only a pub rather than the real mill. Another Bexley photograph is especially interesting, for it shows High Street shops but just misses the very attractive 18th-century Styleman Almshouses. This is just as well, for the protected almshouses remain exactly the same, of course,

whilst the shops have suffered substantial change.

But it is sometimes interesting to see confirmation that a building is virtually unchanged: we find this at Penge, which is often the butt of jokes about suburbia. However, its skyline is a delight, with hints of Oxford, thanks to the huge Watermen's almshouses complex, Queen Adelaide's Cottages and the fine St John's parish church. The interesting architecture is part of the busy High Street, and so it has been enjoyed as part of local daily life for over 150 years.

Sometimes a landmark disappears, as it did in Shortlands: here, the church was a victim of Second World War damage. Nearby Bromley also suffered bomb damage to its fine Kentish church, but the Frith pictures not only show the pre-war church but confirm that the greatest change has been not in war but during the last fifty years. Today a new market place has been inaugurated in the now pedestrianised High Street, where the huge pioneering Churchill Theatre and Library have dictated the new look on the west side.

Even greater change can be found in Croydon, which has become known for its tall buildings transforming this former Surrey coaching town. So dramatic has been the regeneration and growth, that some of the 'new' post-war buildings are already part of our architectural history. It is fascinating to see Archbishop Whitgift's almshouses with trams running past in the Frith photographs. Today, Britain's new modern trams run past the same building. But amid all the change, it is interesting that the Surrey Street market has almost the same crowds and stalls as in 1955.

South of Croydon and Bromley is some of the capital's finest countryside. Here today is Wickham Court, home of Henry VIII's great-aunt, surviving as a college. Nearby are Farnborough, home of Sir John Lubbock who invented Bank Holidays, and Keston Ponds, which were known to local resident William Pitt the Younger.

Still further south is Biggin Hill, where a farmer allowed two flat fields to be used by the pioneers of flying. Biggin Hill Airport played a vital role in the defence of the capital during the Battle of Britain, so it is maybe appropriate that since then it has become part of Greater London. But London has not abused its oversight, as the continued existence of the thatched Spinning Wheel, just inside the London boundary, confirms.

South-east London merges gently with the Garden of England, which in turn still sends its produce daily to the ancient Borough Market in Southwark.

Riverside SE1

The Opening of Tower Bridge 1894 L130019
Tower Bridge was opened by the Prince of Wales in 1894, and
during its first year it was raised more than 6,000 times for ships to
pass through into the Pool of London. The high-level footbridge
was for the use of pedestrians who did not wish to wait for the
road to reopen.

Tower Bridge Completed 1895 L130168
A view of the bridge opening a year after it was inaugurated.
The photographer is standing on Butler's Wharf, where tea, coffee,
cocoa and spices were unloaded from barges. To the right is the
Tower of London on the north bank.

Southwark Findlater's Corner 1897 L130063
A view from London Bridge Station entrance of St Saviour's Collegiate Church, which eight years later became Southwark Cathedral. Findlater's Corner on the left is named after the wine merchant which is now Oddbins. The decorations and temporary tiered seats are for Queen Victoria's Diamond Jubilee procession.

Southwark, St Mary Overie Dock c1875 L130146
The dock takes its name from the nearby Southwark Cathedral, which was the priory of St Mary Overie. The word Overie is a reference to the church being over the water from the City of London. The buildings have gone, but the inlet survives; it is now home to the 'Golden Hinde' replica.

Old Waterloo Bridge 1902 L130155
This is the first Waterloo Bridge, which was opened in 1817 by the Prince Regent, seen from behind Cleopatra's Needle on the north bank. Opposite is the packed working riverside of the South Bank. To the right is the shot tower, which was to become a feature of the Festival of Britain site in 1951.

Lambeth Palace c1955 L1305068
A view of the Archbishop of Canterbury's official residence when Archbishop Geoffrey Fisher, who crowned the Queen, was primate. The gatehouse was completed about 1495. The church on the right is St Mary-at-Lambeth, which has since become the Museum of Garden History. Captain Bligh of mutiny on the Bounty fame is buried in the churchyard.

Elephant & Castle

Elephant and Castle c1890 L130028
The pub which gave the important road junction its name has existed since at least 1765, when a court sat there. The building in this picture was completed in 1816 and demolished in 1898. Heavy bombing during the Second World War led to a redesign of the traffic flow and yet another rebuilding of the pub.

◄ **Camberwell
The Town c1955**
C516001
A break in the traffic
gives a clear view of the
shops on the south side
of Denmark Hill. The
buildings above the
shops survive today, and
the bus stop has moved
only a few yards to the
left. The large building in
the distance beyond
Camberwell Green is the
Father Red Cap pub.

Camberwell

◄ **Camberwell
The Town c1955**

C516003
Camberwell Green is seen from the bottom of Denmark Hill. Approaching is an LCC ambulance; on the left a tram, about to go out of service, heads towards Walworth Road. The impressive building with the word 'Bank' over the door is the Camberwell Green Surgery.

◄ **Camberwell
The Town c1955**

C516004
All the buildings in the picture survive, although the shop fronts have changed. The white and gold-fronted Lyon's tea shop is now an Italian restaurant. The road islands and street furniture have also moved and been changed. Buses run across the recently redundant tram lines.

Peckham

Peckham
Rye Lane c1955 P289001
This view shows the north end of Rye Lane at its junction with
Peckham High Street ahead. The street is now pedestrianised, and
the right-hand side has been rebuilt as the Aylesham Shopping
Centre; but the buildings on the left all remain, with Boots still
occupying the same site.

Dulwich

Dulwich, Dulwich College 1898 42660
The foundation stone was laid in 1866; the buildings were designed by Charles Barry the younger. The money for the buildings was raised by selling land to the railways. The Prince of Wales, the future Edward VII, performed the opening ceremony in 1870.

Dulwich, Dulwich College 1898 42659
Here we see the central block containing the assembly hall. The £100,000 compensation from the railways allowed for a lavish North Italian Renaissance style, and much terracotta was used for the first time on a large building. Pupils who later enjoyed the buildings include the explorer Ernest Shackleton and the novelist P G Woodhouse.

◄ **Dulwich
The Village c1965**
D61008
The view north up the village appears little changed today. To the left, Bartley's is still selling flowers on the corner of Boxall Road. But the post box has crossed the road to be near the new Post Office on the left, and the pillared building on the extreme left is now a Pizza Express.

◀ **Dulwich**
The Village c1965
D61011
Today the trees have matured, and the shop fronts have changed dramatically. However, S G Smith on the left is still at the end of the parade of shops, and still sells cars. At the opposite end, the trees mark the old burial ground beyond the road junction.

▼ **Dulwich**
Dulwich Park c1955
F179011
Dulwich Park opened in 1890 on five fields of former farmland. One gate is named after Lord Rosebury, who performed the opening ceremony, and another after Queen Mary, who came every year to enjoy the display of rhododendrons in bloom. Today the bridge has lost its decoration, but there are still rowing boats.

◀ **Dulwich**
Lordship Lane c1955
D61006
This view looks north from the junction with Dulwich Common. Behind the camera is St Peter's Church, and on the left is the Grove Tavern. Ahead is one of the buses which took over from the trams in 1951, although the tram tracks remained for some time.

◄ **Forest Hill**
The Station and the
Crossroads c1955
F179015
We are looking north
from the bus stop at the
start of Dartmouth Road.
Forest Hill Station is to
the right, and London
Road to the left. Today
the corner shop on the
left is now the Forest Hill
Laundrette. The
interesting station
building on the right has
been rebuilt.

Forest Hill

◀ Forest Hill
The Horniman
Museum c1950

F179003

Tea merchant Frederick Horniman demolished his own home in 1898 to build this museum for the many items he had collected on his world travels. In 1901 the Art Nouveau-style building by C Harrison Townshend was presented to the London County Council. Trams ceased to run past the museum shortly after this picture was taken.

◀ Forest Hill
Devonshire Road c1955

F179017

This picture was taken from a point a few yards further north than No F179015. Ahead is Devonshire Road and the spire of St John's Presbyterian Church; today it has gone to make way for Leyton Court housing, and the congregation worships in the hall behind. A once familiar Ovaltine advertisement can be seen on the wall to the left - and note the Guinness poster.

Forest Hill, Dartmouth Road c1965 F179007
This view north towards Forest Hill Station shows the junction with Derby Hill as it was before the church on the left gave way to the Heron House office block. Today the clock on the right has survived, despite a change of business.

Forest Hill, London Road c1955 F179016
This photograph shows the east end of London Road, with Sainsbury's grocery shop to the right and the Capitol Cinema on the left. Sainsbury's has gone, but the nearby bus stop is in the same position. The cinema is now the Capitol Wetherspoon pub with the bar occupying the stage.

Herne Hill

Herne Hill
The Cross-Roads c1955 H410001
On the left is the magnificent Half Moon pub, which was built in
1896, and ahead is the garage, which remains in business today.
However, the signal box on the line from Blackfriars has gone,
along with the advertising on the railway bridge.

Herne Hill, Half Moon Hill c1955 H410002

Both parades of shops, as well as the residential buildings ahead, would be familiar today. Most of the shop fronts have changed, including that of the pharmacy on the right, which is still trading. The two lamps on the right are part of the Half Moon pub forecourt.

Herne Hill, Railton Road c1955 H410004
Railton Road runs from Brixton and today, at its south end, it continues to be a one-way street. It is unusual that many of the shops have not changed. The laundrette is there today, and The Fruiterers (centre) has become the Fruit Garden. Two doors along to the right, Kennedy's remains, and so does its neighbour Walters the butcher.

Herne Hill
Norwood Road c1955
H410006
At the time of this photograph, Norwood Road still has tramline points at the junction with Dulwich Road on the right. The railing and trees on the right are part of Brockwell Park, and the shops on the far side are under the Herne Hill to Tulse Hill railway line.

Lewisham

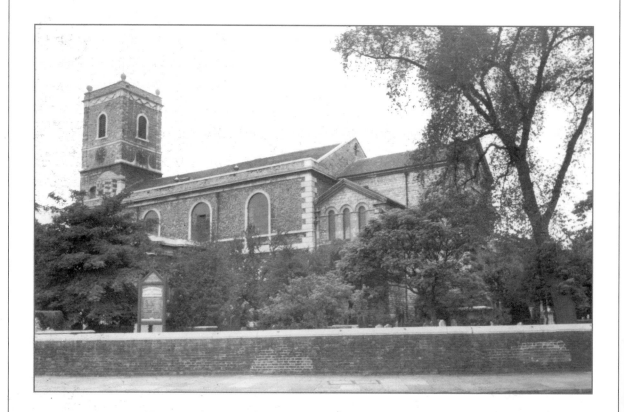

Lewisham
St Mary's Church c1965 L373010
The ancient parish church of Lewisham in the High Street dates
from the late 15th century, although the tower top and the nave
with its tall rounded windows, which we see here, were completed
in 1777. Inside there are monuments added soon after
by Banks and Flaxman.

Catford, Southend

Catford, Southend, The Green Man c1960 C520010
The Green Man, which dates from at least 1600, is no longer a Watney's house but is now branded a Beefeater Steakhouse. Beyond is the former chapel, built in 1824 as Southend Hall, but used by the villagers as a parish church until a new church was built behind.

Catford, Southend, Peter Pan's Pool c1960 C520011
This popular pool is opposite the Green Man, and is now part of the Homebase store. The lake is fed by the River Ravensbourne, which rises at Keston; it once powered two mills here. This pool is the former Lower Mill Pond.

◀ **Greenwich
The Royal Naval
College 1951**
G204021
A closer view of one of
the Royal Naval College
buildings, which today
are the home of the
University of Greenwich
and The Trinity College of
Music. Behind the statue
stands Queen's House,
designed by Inigo Jones
for James I's wife.

Greenwich

◄ **Greenwich
The Royal Naval
College 1951**
G204288
This is the famous view of
the Royal Naval College,
designed by Christopher
Wren in 1695, seen from
the tip of the Isle of
Dogs. To the left and
right there are typical
Thames barges, which
have largely disappeared
from the river today.

◄ **Greenwich
The Observatory c1960**
G204053
Flamsteed House,
designed by Sir
Christopher Wren, was
the Royal Observatory
from 1675 until 1948.
The ball on the roof still
drops at 1pm so that
sailors on the Thames
can set their clocks. The
figure on the right is
crossing the Greenwich
Meridian, which is
marked in the wall and
on the ground.

Greenwich
The Observatory Clock c1960 G204054
This rare 24-hour clock, showing Greenwich Mean Time, is in the wall outside Flamsteed House, the old Royal Observatory. It was placed in the wall in the 1880s with plates showing the standard pre-metric measurements of the period.

Greenwich
A Hokey Pokey Stall 1884 L130110
Children enjoy quickly-melting ice cream on a hot day in Greenwich. Most of the sellers were Italian at this time. The railway posters behind advertise tickets to Brussels and cheap trips to the sea-side every Sunday.

Woolwich

Woolwich
The Ferry c1963 W460028
The 'Ernest Bevin' was one of three new diesel vessels built in
Dundee and delivered in 1963 to replace the paddle steamers
serving the Woolwich Free Ferry, which had run across the Thames
since 1889. Former Foreign Secretary Ernest Bevin was closely
associated with the docks, and was briefly MP for East Woolwich.

Eltham

Eltham
The Church 1900 45831
The building still seemed new to some people at this time, for it
was rebuilt in 1872 on the site of the smaller 17th-century church.
Thomas Doggett, founder of Doggett's Coat & Badge Race for
scullers held annually on the Thames, is buried outside the south
side of the church.

Mottingham

Mottingham
The Memorial c1965 M297010
The focus of Mottingham is the war memorial in the centre of the
road junction. To the right is the steep roof of the Porcupine pub,
which only dates from 1922, although there has been a pub of the
same name here since the 17th century.

Mottingham, Mottingham Road c1960 M297004
This view looks down Mottingham Road towards the war memorial from the corner of Court Road. The RACS shop on the right (the Royal Arsenal Co-operative Society) was a familiar name in most of south-east London's high streets at this time.

Mottingham, The Tarn c1965 M297016
A rustic bridge over the pond at the Tarn park. It is well known for its ice house, which was built in about 1760 for nearby Eltham Lodge. The water, then known as Starbucks Pond, was used for skating by villagers from Eltham and Mottingham.

Mottingham
Mottingham Farm Riding School c1965 M297042
Mottingham Farm, a former dairy farm in Mottingham Lane, has
survived to become a popular stables and riding school; it still
helps to preserve the rural feel of Mottingham, although the A20
and the Dartford Loop railway line are both behind.

Chislehurst

Chislehurst, The Village Sign c1965 C97014
The sign opposite Royal Parade shows Queen Elizabeth I knighting Lord of the Manor Thomas
Walsingham during her visit in 1597. The shield, showing the white horse of Kent, is a reminder
that Chislehurst was in the County of Kent until London extended its boundary in 1965, placing the
village within the London Borough of Bromley.

Chislehurst, High Street c1965 C97025
The Church of the Annunciation can be seen above the small shops. It was built thanks to the profits of the Hymns Ancient & Modern hymn book by the first vicar, Canon Francis Murray. The detached tower, based on Exeter Cathedral's north transept tower, was Murray's memorial; it was completed in 1930, more than thirty years after his death.

Chislehurst, The Rambler's Rest c1965 C97019
The pub stands in its unchanging setting, with only the car giving the hint of a date. The building, which has a split-level bar, owes its rural ambience to its position on the edge of Chislehurst Common. It is handy for commuters, who climb up the hill from the station.

Petts Wood

Petts Wood, The William Willett Sundial c1965 P377004
William Willett, who lived in nearby Chislehurst, had the idea of British Summer Time whilst riding in Petts Wood; he made his proposal public in 1908. The Daylight Bill was passed in 1918, just after Willett's death. His sundial memorial remains unchanged today, although the undergrowth has increased.

Bickley

Bickley
The Church from the South-West 1899 42958
St George's Church was built on the corner of Georges Road, to
the left, and the main Bickley Park Road between 1863 and 1865
as part of a new residential development, which had begun in
1861. Six years after this picture was taken,
the tower and spire were rebuilt.

Belvedere
Nuxley Road c1955
B704016
Another view down Nuxley Road taken a little later in the 1950s. Next to the Royal Arsenal Co-operative Society greengrocer's shop on the right is Belvedere Baptist Church, advertising its Harvest Festival, while opposite is another greengrocer - but today both have gone. However, the Co-op still retains the shop on the extreme left.

Belvedere

◀ **Belvedere**
Nuxley Road c1950
B704007
The spire of the mid-Victorian All Saints Church is the focal point of this view south down Nuxley Road. Today the pub on the right displays a pictorial sign, and the increase in car ownership has caused traffic calming measures to be introduced.

◀ **Belvedere**
The Fountain and the Children's Pond c1950
B704001
The Belvedere paddling pool lies on the corner of the main Woolwich Road and Heron Hill. Today the scene is similar when it is filled with water between June and August. However, the fountain has been reduced in height by a third, thus losing the attractive decoration.

◀ **Erith**
High Street c1955 E58013
The climax of the High
Street is the 1892 Cross
Keys pub building in the
centre of the photograph.
To the right is the tall White
Hart, completed in 1902.
Today the Locomotive on
the left, along with most of
the street, has gone. The
narrow turning on the right
is now the wide Wharfeside
Close leading to the pier.

Erith

◄ Erith
The River c1965
E58038
Here we see the Erith riverside before the flood defences and the Thames Path were built. At this time, too, the Rainham Marshes shore on the Essex bank opposite had not yet been raised by landfill. But the upstream skyline is little changed today.

◄ Erith
High Street c1955
E58012
This street was lost in 1968 when the controversial Town Centre development by the architect Richard Seifert was completed. The successor complex had provision for the street market stalls seen in the picture, but the shopping focus has recently moved again with the opening of a Morrisons on the riverside.

Erith, Walnut Tree Road c1955 E58008
A London Transport trolley bus picks up passengers at the side of Erith Town Hall, which had been built in 1938 for Erith Urban District Council. Its successor, Erith Borough Council, met here until 1965, when Bexley Council embraced Erith. The building remains a council office; it recently had a extra floor added.

Erith, New Flats c1960 E58042
Boundary Street was still a rough road when these flats were new. Today the flats' distinctive roofline has been renewed; the approach road is metalled now, and there are houses to the left. Only the last two far sections of the pub garden wall on the right survive.

Bexley

Bexley
North Cray Road c1965 B83061
The southern approach to Old Bexley, at the beginning of the High
Street, is dominated by Bexley's ancient church on the corner of
Manor Road. Today the village is no longer announced by a sign
with the Kentish white horse, and the church is hidden by a tree.

Bexley, The Church 1900 45839
The 13th-century flint Kentish church with its octagonal tower still looks in good condition in this picture taken just 17 years after its restoration. Today the lamp post has gone, but the bollard in the foreground remains.

Bexley, The Old Mill c1955 B83025
A decade after this photograph was taken, the picturesque weatherboarded mill on the River Cray was burnt down. It has been replaced by a convincing replica, and is now known as the Old Mill restaurant.

Bexley
High Street c1955 B83043
A view north-east along the village high street, with the stone spire
of St John's Church, completed in 1882, seen ahead. On the left
we can see one of the once-familiar police boxes; today it has
made way for a supermarket on the corner of the station approach,
which is being crossed here by a man with a bicycle.

▼ Bexley, The King's Head Inn c1955 B83042

This 16th-century timber-framed inn, with oak beams inside, stands in the heart of Old Bexley village. The sign shows a figure which appears to be a Hanoverian king. The forecourt is no longer a car park, but has tables for summer eating and drinking.

▼ Bexley, High Street c1965 B83065

This photograph featuring the forecourt of the King's Head was taken ten years after No B83042. It has become a Courage pub, with a new picture of the King on the inn sign. Today, however, the king is Henry VIII. Ahead is the junction with Bourne Road on the left.

▲ Bexley Bourne Road c1955

B83067

We are looking north at the start of Bourne Road, which links Old Bexley with Crayford. The public library is on the left, and a Post Office on the right. The scene today is almost the same, except that the Post Office has gone, leaving a post box at the side.

**Bexley
Hall Place c1955**

B83050

Hall Place was built in 1537 for former Lord Mayor of London Sir John Champneys, who may have taken advantage of the dissolution of the monasteries to obtain the stone. The brick extension was added in 1649. It was a boarding school in the 19th century, and until recently it was Bexley's Local History Museum.

◀ **Beckenham Christ Church 1899**

43389

The Early English-style brick Christ Church in Fairfield Road was just 23 years old at the time of this photograph. On its 25th anniversary in 1901, a school was added. The foreground was soon filled with a terrace of houses, which now includes the Liberal Club.

Beckenham

◀ Beckenham
Beckenham Place 1899

43383

Beckenham Place was bought and enhanced in 1773 as a residence by the local benefactor John Cator, who gave his name to Cator Park. His arms are above the portico, which came from the demolished Wricklemarsh House at Blackheath Park in 1787. Beckenham Place has been a school, a sanatorium, and a clubhouse for the golf course which now occupies the grounds.

◀ Beckenham
High Street c1965

B46075

Tesco, then offering the once very popular Green Shield Stamps, has today moved to a larger site. But Beckenham Toys is still in the High Street. The car on the left is leaving Village Way, and the bus is heading for the junction with Croydon Road.

Beckenham, Church Hill c1965 B46053
The tower of St George's church dominates the scene, which today is little changed. The buildings all remain, apart from the one to the right of the church, but new traffic lights control much heavier traffic.

Beckenham, The Cottage Hospital 1899 43395
The original 1877 Cottage Hospital building survives in Croydon Road as part of Beckenham Hospital. The creeper has been removed, and the chimneys have been cut down, but behind a new low wall the building remains an important local landmark.

Penge

Penge
Holy Trinity Church 1899 43559
Twenty years after they were planted, the church's trees begin
to look mature. Although the church had been opened in 1878,
the unusual stunted pyramid spire was added later in 1883.
At the beginning of the century this area was still a hamlet,
with no need for a large church.

▼ **Penge, Waterman's Asylum 1899** 43827

In 1840 Queen Adelaide gave 100 guineas towards the building of these almshouses for 60 former Thames watermen. The view is little changed; with St John's church next door, the buildings give the High Street an unusual character. Nearby is the King William Naval Asylum for widows of naval officers, which was built during the same period.

▼ **Penge, The Alexandra Recreation Ground 1899** 43826

Three gardeners are at work in the park at the end of the Victorian era. Ahead is St John's church across the High Street. Today the park layout is the same, but the low fences and most of the seats have gone. The park entrance in the distance has become the war memorial.

▲ **Penge High Street c1955**
P26002

The Police Station on the right is on the corner of Green Lane. On the left is one of the many branches of United Dairies, which also had an extensive network of doorstep delivery rounds. Today the shop is a solicitor's office. The Essoldo has given way to Boots and the entrance to the Blenheim Centre.

◀
**Penge
High Street c1960**

P26014

Today Glass the butcher
is still on the corner of
Southey Street, but Boots
has given way to Superdrug
by moving to the Essoldo
site across the road. Here,
where the road widens by
the Penge Lane junction,
the area has now become
a town square with a new
clock as focus.

◀ **Bromley
Shortlands
Westmorland Road 1899**
42952
We are looking at Numbers 30 and 32 Westmorland Road. Today the houses are little changed, although number 30 has had a loft conversion. The further house, on the corner of Queen Anne Avenue, survives, but has now lost its finials. The lamp post has given way to a bus stop in this now busy road.

Shortlands

▲ Bromley
Shortlands 1899
42942
The view looks from Martin's Hill across the valley of the Ravensbourne River. Ahead we can see the pumping station chimney. Behind on the skyline is the spire of the just-completed St Mary's church in Shortlands, which was lost when it was hit by a German bomb in the Second World War.

Bromley ▶
Shortlands Church 1899
42954
The 1870 stone St Mary's church, at the end of Church Road, looking clean and new just a decade after being enlarged. The church was hit by a bomb during the Second World War and was rebuilt to a new design in the 1950s.

◀ **Bromley
Palace Park 1899**
42950
The Bishops of Rochester,
who owned the manor of
Bromley from 862 until
1845, maintained a palace
here from the 10th century.
The grounds became a park
in the Victorian era, and
more recently the 18th-
century Old Palace has been
enlarged to become part of
the civic centre.

Bromley

◄ Bromley
The Parish Church
and the Lychgate 1899

42938

The parish church of
St Peter and St Paul had
been rebuilt in 1790 as a
typical Kentish church.
Following bombing
during the Second World
War, the familiar tower is
today attached to a new
church. The wall
survives, but the
lychgate has a new
position.

◄ Bromley
The College 1899

43369

The College was
founded in the late 17th
century by Bishop
Warner of Rochester as
almshouses for 'twentie
poore widows of
orthodox and loyall
clergiemen'. The
building, one of the
oldest of its kind in
England, remains little
changed and continues
its original function.

▼ Bromley, Market Square c1955 B226010

An easterly view towards Widmore Road, the outfitters on the corner is today a café. The main building on the left has gone, and the Freeman, Hardy Willis shoe shop on the extreme left is now Jessops. Buses still run here past the now pedestrianised entrance to the High Street where the photographer is standing.

▼ Bromley, Market Square c1965 B226135

This view also looks east, but it was taken ten years after photograph No B226010. Today the Midland Bank is still on the right, although its name is now HSBC. Tip Top Bakeries at the far end is now a shoe shop. Bromley's first market charter was granted in 1205.

▲ Bromley High Street c1955
B226052

A view of the parade of shops next to Bromley South Station on the right. The second shop from the station, Kennedy's pie shop, remains; the words 'Kennedy's Sausages' are still on the facade above the shop front. Further up the gentle hill, Dewhurst's now a hairdresser, is receiving a delivery of meat.

◀ **Bromley**
High Street c1965
B226053
This view shows the High Street from a position further north a decade later than photograph No B226052. On the left is Elmfield Road, which now marks the edge of the Glades Shopping Centre. The Eastern Gas Board showroom building has been replaced, and now The Pier and Boots occupy the corner.

Bromley
High Street c1960
B226055
Here we see the north end of Bromley High Street before it was pedestrianised to become the new market site. Today the buildings on the left have changed, and now include the entrance to the Churchill Theatre. Barratts shoe shop still occupies the shop in the 1887 Aberdeen Building to the right.

Bromley, The Park c1965 B226067
The tower of Bromley Parish Church rises behind Church House Gardens. Today the pond has a fence around it, and the park is still very well cared for, with more flower beds in the lawn.

Bromley, The Floral Clock, Library Gardens c1960 B226029
Library Gardens survives as part of a larger park behind the Churchill Theatre, which incorporates the modern library. The theatre, the first in Britain to have no aisles, is the successor to the New Theatre, which was gutted by fire.

West Wickham

Beckenham
Wickham Court 1899 43397
Today the mansion is free of the creeper which hid the fine Tudor
brickwork. This was the home of Sir Henry Heydon; he married
Anne Boleyn, great-aunt of Henry VIII's queen of the same name.
The house, now part of St John Rigby College, is an example of an
early grand domestic house.

Farnborough

Farnborough
High Elms Road c1965 F185032
This former farmhouse is now known as The Clock House because
of the clock on the far side. In the garden stands a small octagonal
building, dating from about 1850 and looking like a summer house,
which housed a horse wheel to pump water up from a well into a
tank in the tiny building's roof.

Keston

Keston
The Fishponds 1899 42964
The three Keston Ponds are the source of the River Ravensbourne, which
enters the River Thames as Deptford Creek. Keston Common remains little
changed; its Caesar's Well feeds the ponds, and there are ancient
earthworks on the common. It is still a place of recreation, just as it was in
this picture, where children play with a model sailing boat.

Biggin Hill

Biggin Hill
The Old Jail Inn c1950 B705017
The pub, once two Kentish cottages, remains little changed along
the hedged lane. Local Westerham ales were once served here.
The origin of the name is uncertain, but prisoners being
transported from the London courts to Maidstone Prison
may have been lodged here.

Biggin Hill
The Valley c1950 B705007
The lanes to the west of Main Road and the airfield are in a valley,
where some of the earliest dwellings appeared early in the last
century. They were mainly shacks and cottages, and a few remain
in the now residential roads like Norheads Lane.

Biggin Hill, The Spinning Wheel c1955 B705028
The thatched tea-room at Hawley's Corner, a five-way junction, was a popular stop for motorists on the road from Westerham. In 1955 this was part of Kent, but ten years later London was extended - now the Spinning Wheel Restaurant is just a few yards inside Greater London .

Biggin Hill, The Airport c1965 B705075
The airport's beginnings were before the First World War, when one of the large fields belonging to Cudham Hall Farm was used for landing early aircraft. In the Second World War the airfield played an important role in the Battle of Britain.

Coulsdon

Coulsdon
The Sign Post, Farthing Down c1965 C165052
Farthing Down was bought in 1883 by the Corporation of London
to safeguard the green viewpoint between Old Coulsdon in the east
and Coulsdon on the Brighton road in the valley to the west. Now
this countryside is on the very edge of Greater London.

Croydon

**Croydon
North End 1896** 38651
The brand-new tower of the Town
Hall can be seen above the far
shops in North End, which today is
a pedestrianised road. The
buildings on the left have given
way to the Whitgift Shopping
Centre, which was named after the
Archbishop who had the hospital
built at the junction ahead.

Croydon
The Municipal Buildings 1896 38650
The magnificent Croydon Town Hall in Katharine Street is photographed in the year of its completion. The architect was Charles Henman junior, and the building work took four years. Croydon's population had grown during the century from 5,000 to over 100,000. Henman also designed St Paul's in South Croydon which opened a decade later.

Croydon, Main Street c1950 C201018
Another view south down North End taken just over half a century after picture No 38651. Now the tram lines have been doubled, and buses have appeared. To the left is the Odeon cinema: it advertises Glynis Johns in 'Miranda'.

Croydon, High Street c1950 C201025
A view north up the High Street, which bears slightly to the right. Ahead is the entrance to Surrey Street by a corner building - it still survives. There are two motor bikes with side cars in the picture, which would not have been unusual at this time.

Croydon, Surrey Street c1955 C201051

This has been a market area for 700 years; it once operated under a charter from the Archbishop of Canterbury, who lived at nearby Croydon Palace. Today it remains just as busy and popular for fruit and vegetables, despite the many supermarkets now nearby.

Croydon, Church Street c1955 C201005

A view north up Church Street with Surrey Street Market to the right. Ahead at the top of the hill is Whitgift Hospital, which was built as a home for 16 men and 16 women in 1596 by the Archbishop Whitgift. The building then marked the edge of the town.

Index

Frith Book Co Titles

www.francisfrith.co.uk

The Frith Book Company publishes over 100 new titles each year. A selection of those currently available are listed below. For latest catalogue please contact Frith Book Co.

Town Books 96 pages, approx 100 photos. County and Themed Books 128 pages, approx 150 photos (unless specified). All titles hardback laminated case and jacket except those indicated pb (paperback)

Title	ISBN	Price		Title	ISBN	Price
Amersham, Chesham & Rickmansworth (pb)				Derby (pb)	1-85937-367-4	£9.99
	1-85937-340-2	£9.99		Derbyshire (pb)	1-85937-196-5	£9.99
Ancient Monuments & Stone Circles	1-85937-143-4	£17.99		Devon (pb)	1-85937-297-x	£9.99
Aylesbury (pb)	1-85937-227-9	£9.99		Dorset (pb)	1-85937-269-4	£9.99
Bakewell	1-85937-113-2	£12.99		Dorset Churches	1-85937-172-8	£17.99
Barnstaple (pb)	1-85937-300-3	£9.99		Dorset Coast (pb)	1-85937-299-6	£9.99
Bath (pb)	1-85937419-0	£9.99		Dorset Living Memories	1-85937-210-4	£14.99
Bedford (pb)	1-85937-205-8	£9.99		Down the Severn	1-85937-118-3	£14.99
Berkshire (pb)	1-85937-191-4	£9.99		Down the Thames (pb)	1-85937-278-3	£9.99
Berkshire Churches	1-85937-170-1	£17.99		Down the Trent	1-85937-311-9	£14.99
Blackpool (pb)	1-85937-382-8	£9.99		Dublin (pb)	1-85937-231-7	£9.99
Bognor Regis (pb)	1-85937-431-x	£9.99		East Anglia (pb)	1-85937-265-1	£9.99
Bournemouth	1-85937-067-5	£12.99		East London	1-85937-080-2	£14.99
Bradford (pb)	1-85937-204-x	£9.99		East Sussex	1-85937-130-2	£14.99
Brighton & Hove(pb)	1-85937-192-2	£8.99		Eastbourne	1-85937-061-6	£12.99
Bristol (pb)	1-85937-264-3	£9.99		Edinburgh (pb)	1-85937-193-0	£8.99
British Life A Century Ago (pb)	1-85937-213-9	£9.99		England in the 1880s	1-85937-331-3	£17.99
Buckinghamshire (pb)	1-85937-200-7	£9.99		English Castles (pb)	1-85937-434-4	£9.99
Camberley (pb)	1-85937-222-8	£9.99		English Country Houses	1-85937-161-2	£17.99
Cambridge (pb)	1-85937-422-0	£9.99		Essex (pb)	1-85937-270-8	£9.99
Cambridgeshire (pb)	1-85937-420-4	£9.99		Exeter	1-85937-126-4	£12.99
Canals & Waterways (pb)	1-85937-291-0	£9.99		Exmoor	1-85937-132-9	£14.99
Canterbury Cathedral (pb)	1-85937-179-5	£9.99		Falmouth	1-85937-066-7	£12.99
Cardiff (pb)	1-85937-093-4	£9.99		Folkestone (pb)	1-85937-124-8	£9.99
Carmarthenshire	1-85937-216-3	£14.99		Glasgow (pb)	1-85937-190-6	£9.99
Chelmsford (pb)	1-85937-310-0	£9.99		Gloucestershire	1-85937-102-7	£14.99
Cheltenham (pb)	1-85937-095-0	£9.99		Great Yarmouth (pb)	1-85937-426-3	£9.99
Cheshire (pb)	1-85937-271-6	£9.99		Greater Manchester (pb)	1-85937-266-x	£9.99
Chester	1-85937-090-x	£12.99		Guildford (pb)	1-85937-410-7	£9.99
Chesterfield	1-85937-378-x	£9.99		Hampshire (pb)	1-85937-279-1	£9.99
Chichester (pb)	1-85937-228-7	£9.99		Hampshire Churches (pb)	1-85937-207-4	£9.99
Colchester (pb)	1-85937-188-4	£8.99		Harrogate	1-85937-423-9	£9.99
Cornish Coast	1-85937-163-9	£14.99		Hastings & Bexhill (pb)	1-85937-131-0	£9.99
Cornwall (pb)	1-85937-229-5	£9.99		Heart of Lancashire (pb)	1-85937-197-3	£9.99
Cornwall Living Memories	1-85937-248-1	£14.99		Helston (pb)	1-85937-214-7	£9.99
Cotswolds (pb)	1-85937-230-9	£9.99		Hereford (pb)	1-85937-175-2	£9.99
Cotswolds Living Memories	1-85937-255-4	£14.99		Herefordshire	1-85937-174-4	£14.99
County Durham	1-85937-123-x	£14.99		Hertfordshire (pb)	1-85937-247-3	£9.99
Croydon Living Memories	1-85937-162-0	£9.99		Horsham (pb)	1-85937-432-8	£9.99
Cumbria	1-85937-101-9	£14.99		Humberside	1-85937-215-5	£14.99
Dartmoor	1-85937-145-0	£14.99		Hythe, Romney Marsh & Ashford	1-85937-256-2	£9.99

Available from your local bookshop or from the publisher

Frith Book Co Titles (continued)

Title	ISBN	Price	Title	ISBN	Price
Ipswich (pb)	1-85937-424-7	£9.99	St Ives (pb)	1-85937415-8	£9.99
Ireland (pb)	1-85937-181-7	£9.99	Scotland (pb)	1-85937-182-5	£9.99
Isle of Man (pb)	1-85937-268-6	£9.99	Scottish Castles (pb)	1-85937-323-2	£9.99
Isles of Scilly	1-85937-136-1	£14.99	Sevenoaks & Tunbridge	1-85937-057-8	£12.99
Isle of Wight (pb)	1-85937-429-8	£9.99	Sheffield, South Yorks (pb)	1-85937-267-8	£9.99
Isle of Wight Living Memories	1-85937-304-6	£14.99	Shrewsbury (pb)	1-85937-325-9	£9.99
Kent (pb)	1-85937-189-2	£9.99	Shropshire (pb)	1-85937-326-7	£9.99
Kent Living Memories	1-85937-125-6	£14.99	Somerset	1-85937-153-1	£14.99
Lake District (pb)	1-85937-275-9	£9.99	South Devon Coast	1-85937-107-8	£14.99
Lancaster, Morecambe & Heysham (pb)	1-85937-233-3	£9.99	South Devon Living Memories	1-85937-168-x	£14.99
Leeds (pb)	1-85937-202-3	£9.99	South Hams	1-85937-220-1	£14.99
Leicester	1-85937-073-x	£12.99	Southampton (pb)	1-85937-427-1	£9.99
Leicestershire (pb)	1-85937-185-x	£9.99	Southport (pb)	1-85937-425-5	£9.99
Lincolnshire (pb)	1-85937-433-6	£9.99	Staffordshire	1-85937-047-0	£12.99
Liverpool & Merseyside (pb)	1-85937-234-1	£9.99	Stratford upon Avon	1-85937-098-5	£12.99
London (pb)	1-85937-183-3	£9.99	Suffolk (pb)	1-85937-221-x	£9.99
Ludlow (pb)	1-85937-176-0	£9.99	Suffolk Coast	1-85937-259-7	£14.99
Luton (pb)	1-85937-235-x	£9.99	Surrey (pb)	1-85937-240-6	£9.99
Maidstone	1-85937-056-x	£14.99	Sussex (pb)	1-85937-184-1	£9.99
Manchester (pb)	1-85937-198-1	£9.99	Swansea (pb)	1-85937-167-1	£9.99
Middlesex	1-85937-158-2	£14.99	Tees Valley & Cleveland	1-85937-211-2	£14.99
New Forest	1-85937-128-0	£14.99	Thanet (pb)	1-85937-116-7	£9.99
Newark (pb)	1-85937-366-6	£9.99	Tiverton (pb)	1-85937-178-7	£9.99
Newport, Wales (pb)	1-85937-258-9	£9.99	Torbay	1-85937-063-2	£12.99
Newquay (pb)	1-85937-421-2	£9.99	Truro	1-85937-147-7	£12.99
Norfolk (pb)	1-85937-195-7	£9.99	Victorian and Edwardian Cornwall	1-85937-252-x	£14.99
Norfolk Living Memories	1-85937-217-1	£14.99	Victorian & Edwardian Devon	1-85937-253-8	£14.99
Northamptonshire	1-85937-150-7	£14.99	Victorian & Edwardian Kent	1-85937-149-3	£14.99
Northumberland Tyne & Wear (pb)	1-85937-281-3	£9.99	Vic & Ed Maritime Album	1-85937-144-2	£17.99
North Devon Coast	1-85937-146-9	£14.99	Victorian and Edwardian Sussex	1-85937-157-4	£14.99
North Devon Living Memories	1-85937-261-9	£14.99	Victorian & Edwardian Yorkshire	1-85937-154-x	£14.99
North London	1-85937-206-6	£14.99	Victorian Seaside	1-85937-159-0	£17.99
North Wales (pb)	1-85937-298-8	£9.99	Villages of Devon (pb)	1-85937-293-7	£9.99
North Yorkshire (pb)	1-85937-236-8	£9.99	Villages of Kent (pb)	1-85937-294-5	£9.99
Norwich (pb)	1-85937-194-9	£8.99	Villages of Sussex (pb)	1-85937-295-3	£9.99
Nottingham (pb)	1-85937-324-0	£9.99	Warwickshire (pb)	1-85937-203-1	£9.99
Nottinghamshire (pb)	1-85937-187-6	£9.99	Welsh Castles (pb)	1-85937-322-4	£9.99
Oxford (pb)	1-85937-411-5	£9.99	West Midlands (pb)	1-85937-289-9	£9.99
Oxfordshire (pb)	1-85937-430-1	£9.99	West Sussex	1-85937-148-5	£14.99
Peak District (pb)	1-85937-280-5	£9.99	West Yorkshire (pb)	1-85937-201-5	£9.99
Penzance	1-85937-069-1	£12.99	Weymouth (pb)	1-85937-209-0	£9.99
Peterborough (pb)	1-85937-219-8	£9.99	Wiltshire (pb)	1-85937-277-5	£9.99
Piers	1-85937-237-6	£17.99	Wiltshire Churches (pb)	1-85937-171-x	£9.99
Plymouth	1-85937-119-1	£12.99	Wiltshire Living Memories	1-85937-245-7	£14.99
Poole & Sandbanks (pb)	1-85937-251-1	£9.99	Winchester (pb)	1-85937-428-x	£9.99
Preston (pb)	1-85937-212-0	£9.99	Windmills & Watermills	1-85937-242-2	£17.99
Reading (pb)	1-85937-238-4	£9.99	Worcester (pb)	1-85937-165-5	£9.99
Romford (pb)	1-85937-319-4	£9.99	Worcestershire	1-85937-152-3	£14.99
Salisbury (pb)	1-85937-239-2	£9.99	York (pb)	1-85937-199-x	£9.99
Scarborough (pb)	1-85937-379-8	£9.99	Yorkshire (pb)	1-85937-186-8	£9.99
St Albans (pb)	1-85937-341-0	£9.99	Yorkshire Living Memories	1-85937-166-3	£14.99

See Frith books on the internet www.francisfrith.co.uk

FRITH PRODUCTS & SERVICES

Francis Frith would doubtless be pleased to know that the pioneering publishing venture he started in 1860 still continues today. A hundred and forty years later, The Francis Frith Collection continues in the same innovative tradition and is now one of the foremost publishers of vintage photographs in the world. Some of the current activities include:

Interior Decoration

Today Frith's photographs can be seen framed and as giant wall murals in thousands of pubs, restaurants, hotels, banks, retail stores and other public buildings throughout the country. In every case they enhance the unique local atmosphere of the places they depict and provide reminders of gentler days in an increasingly busy and frenetic world.

Product Promotions

Frith products are used by many major companies to promote the sales of their own products or to reinforce their own history and heritage. Frith promotions have been used by Hovis bread, Courage beers, Scots Porage Oats, Colman's mustard, Cadbury's foods, Mellow Birds coffee, Dunhill pipe tobacco, Guinness, and Bulmer's Cider.

Genealogy and Family History

As the interest in family history and roots grows world-wide, more and more people are turning to Frith's photographs of Great Britain for images of the towns, villages and streets where their ancestors lived; and, of course, photographs of the churches and chapels where their ancestors were christened, married and buried are an essential part of every genealogy tree and family album.

Frith Products

All Frith photographs are available Framed or just as Mounted Prints and Posters (size 23 x 16 inches). These may be ordered from the address below. From time to time other products - Address Books, Calendars, Table Mats, etc - are available.

The Internet

Already twenty thousand Frith photographs can be viewed and purchased on the internet through the Frith websites and a myriad of partner sites.

For more detailed information on Frith companies and products, look at these sites:

www.francisfrith.co.uk
www.francisfrith.com
(for North American visitors)

See the complete list of Frith Books at:

www.francisfrith.co.uk

This web site is regularly updated with the latest list of publications from the Frith Book Company. If you wish to buy books relating to another part of the country that your local bookshop does not stock, you may purchase on-line.

For further information, trade, or author enquiries please contact us at the address below:
The Francis Frith Collection, Frith's Barn, Teffont, Salisbury, Wiltshire, England SP3 5QP.
Tel: +44 (0)1722 716 376 Fax: +44 (0)1722 716 881 Email: sales@francisfrith.co.uk

See Frith books on the internet www.francisfrith.co.uk

TO RECEIVE YOUR FREE MOUNTED PRINT

Mounted Print
Overall size 14 x 11 inches

Cut out this Voucher and return it with your remittance for £1.95 to cover postage and handling, to UK addresses. For overseas addresses please include £4.00 post and handling. Choose any photograph included in this book. Your SEPIA print will be A4 in size, and mounted in a cream mount with burgundy rule line, overall size 14 x 11 inches.

Order additional Mounted Prints at HALF PRICE (only £7.49 each*)

If there are further pictures you would like to order, possibly as gifts for friends and family, purchase them at half price (no additional postage and handling required).

Have your Mounted Prints framed*

For an additional £14.95 per print you can have your chosen Mounted Print framed in an elegant polished wood and gilt moulding, overall size 16 x 13 inches (no additional postage and handling required).

---

* IMPORTANT!
These special prices are only available if ordered using the original voucher on this page (no copies permitted) and at the same time as your free Mounted Print, for delivery to the same address

---

Frith Collectors' Guild

From time to time we publish a magazine of news and stories about Frith photographs and further special offers of Frith products. If you would like 12 months FREE membership, please return this form.

Send completed forms to:
**The Francis Frith Collection,
Frith's Barn, Teffont, Salisbury,
Wiltshire SP3 5QP**

Voucher for FREE and Reduced Price Frith Prints

Picture no.	Page number	Qty	Mounted @ £7.49	Framed + £14.95	Total Cost
		1	**Free of charge***	£	£
			£7.49	£	£
			£7.49	£	£
			£7.49	£	£
			£7.49	£	£
			£7.49	£	£

Please allow 28 days for delivery	*** Post & handling**	£1.95
Book Title	**Total Order Cost**	£

Please do not photocopy this voucher. Only the original is valid, so please cut it out and return it to us.

I enclose a cheque / postal order for £ . . . .
made payable to 'The Francis Frith Collection'
OR please debit my Mastercard / Visa / Switch / Amex card
(credit cards please on all overseas orders)

Number . . . .

Issue No (Switch only) . . . . Valid from (Amex/Switch) . . . .

Expires . . . . Signature . . . .

Name Mr/Mrs/Ms . . . .

Address . . . .

. . . .

. . . . Postcode . . . .

Daytime Tel No . . . . Valid to 31/12/02

The Francis Frith Collectors' Guild

Please enrol me as a member for 12 months free of charge.

Name Mr/Mrs/Ms . . . .

Address . . . .

. . . .

. . . . Postcode . . . .

Would you like to find out more about Francis Frith?

We have recently recruited some entertaining speakers who are happy to visit local groups, clubs and societies to give an illustrated talk documenting Frith's travels and photographs. If you are a member of such a group and are interested in hosting a presentation, we would love to hear from you.

Our speakers bring with them a small selection of our local town and county books, together with sample prints. They are happy to take orders. A small proportion of the order value is donated to the group who have hosted the presentation. The talks are therefore an excellent way of fundraising for small groups and societies.

Can you help us with information about any of the Frith photographs in this book?

We are gradually compiling an historical record for each of the photographs in the Frith archive. It is always fascinating to find out the names of the people shown in the pictures, as well as insights into the shops, buildings and other features depicted.

If you recognize anyone in the photographs in this book, or if you have information not already included in the author's caption, do let us know. We would love to hear from you, and will try to publish it in future books or articles.

Our production team

Frith books are produced by a small dedicated team at offices in the converted Grade II listed 18th-century barn at Teffont near Salisbury, illustrated above. Most have worked with the Frith Collection for many years. All have in common one quality: they have a passion for the Frith Collection. The team is constantly expanding, but currently includes:

Jason Buck, John Buck, Douglas Burns, Heather Crisp, Isobel Hall, Rob Hames, Hazel Heaton, Peter Horne, James Kinnear, Tina Leary, Hannah Marsh, Eliza Sackett, Terence Sackett, Sandra Sanger, Shelley Tolcher, Susanna Walker, Clive Wathen and Jenny Wathen.